Dances of Time

Bob Chilcott

for SATB chorus and piano or orchestra

Contents

MUSIC DEPARTMENT

OXFORD
UNIVERSITY PRESS

Composer's note

I am very fortunate to have known Brian Kay for almost all my life, since being a chorister at King's College, Cambridge, while he was a bass choral scholar. Brian has had a fruitful life working in the world of music, particularly excelling in the encouragement and development of amateur choir singing. When Brian and the Leith Hill Musical Festival asked me to write a piece in celebration of his twentieth season as Festival Conductor, the key thing for me was to find the right texts for the occasion. I decided to look for texts that reflected not only Brian's spirit but also the idea that, despite the passing of time, music and singing can help us to live in and celebrate the present. The first of the five texts, by King Henry VIII, tells of the joy of good company and friends. The second, by Thomas Carlyle, reflects in a wistful but positive way on the hope of the new day. Robert Herrick's 'Gather ye rosebuds' is a plea to us all to live life in the moment and not to procrastinate! In the fourth movement, verses from Ecclesiastes remind us that with the passing of time comes not only thankfulness, but also reflection and hope for the future. The piece ends with a setting of a poem by Sara Teasdale that brims with energy and positivity, and includes perhaps one of the most powerful mantras for choir singers and lovers of good life: 'For one white singing hour of peace count many a year of strife well lost.'

Duration: *c.*15 minutes

An accompaniment for orchestra (2 fl, 2 ob, 2 cl, 2 bsn, 2 hn, 2 tpt, timp, 2 perc, str) is available on hire/rental from the publisher or appropriate agent.

OXFORD
UNIVERSITY PRESS

Great Clarendon Street, Oxford OX2 6DP,
United Kingdom

© *Oxford University Press 2015*

Bob Chilcott has asserted his right under the Copyright, Designs and Patents Act, 1988, to be identified as the Composer of this Work

First published 2015

ISBN 978-0-19-340060-3

Music origination by Katie Johnston
Printed in Great Britain on acid-free paper by Halstan & Co. Ltd, Amersham, Bucks.

Dances of Time

BOB CHILCOTT

1. Pastime with good company

King Henry VIII (1491–1547)

13

heart is set:_____ All good - ly sport for my com-fort, who shall me

18

S.
A.

let?_____ Some dal - li - ance,

T.
B.

Youth must have__ some dal - li - ance, of good or ill__ some

23

some pas - tance; me-thinks then best, best:_____ For

pas - tance; Com - pa-ny__ me-thinks then best, All thoughts and fan - cies to di-gest: For

Com - pa - ny___ is good and ill but ev -'ry man___ hath his free will. The

best en - sue, the worst es - chew, my mind shall be:___ Vir - tue to use, vice

to re - fuse, thus shall I use___ me.___

2. Today

Thomas Carlyle (1795–1881)

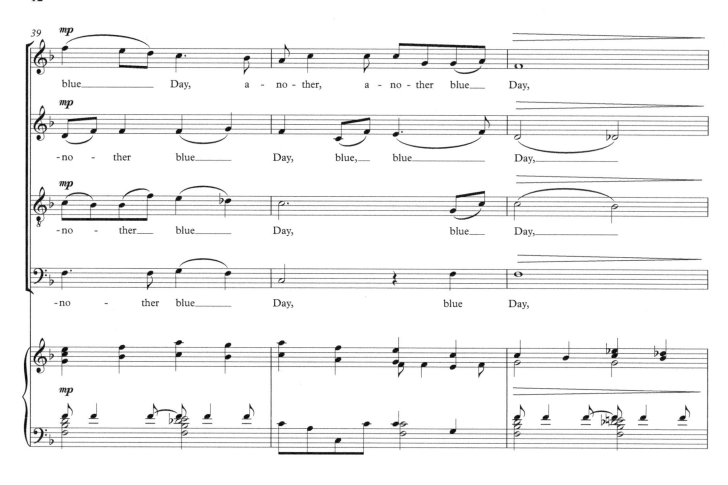

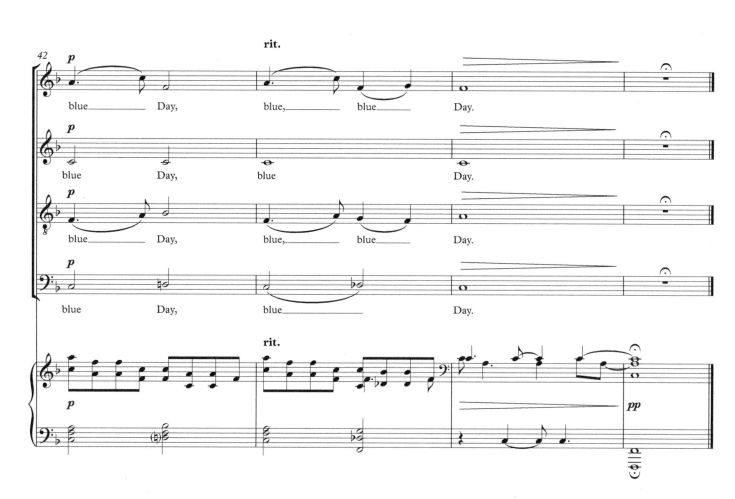

3. Gather ye rosebuds

Robert Herrick (1591–1674)

this__ same flow'r that smiles to - day_____ To - mor - row will be

dy - ing,_____ dy - ing._____

S.
A.

__ The glo - rious lamp_ of heav'n, the sun, The high - er he's a - get - ting,__ The

T.
B.

soon - er will his race be run, And near - er he's to set - ting. That age is best which

is the first, When youth and blood are warm - er; But be - ing spent, the worse, and worst Times

still suc - ceed the for - mer, the for - mer,

the for - mer.

Then be___ not coy, but

use your time,___ And while___ ye may, go mar - ry:___

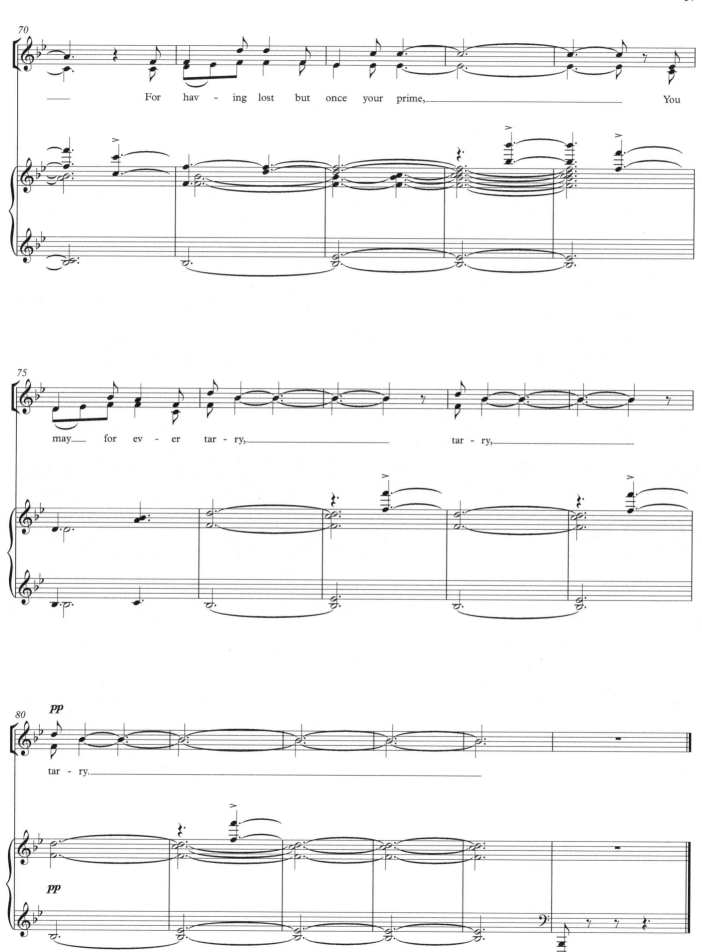

For hav - ing lost but once your prime,_____ You

may___ for ev - er tar - ry,_____ tar - ry,_____

pp

tar - ry._____

4. To every thing there is a season

Ecclesiastes 3: 1–8

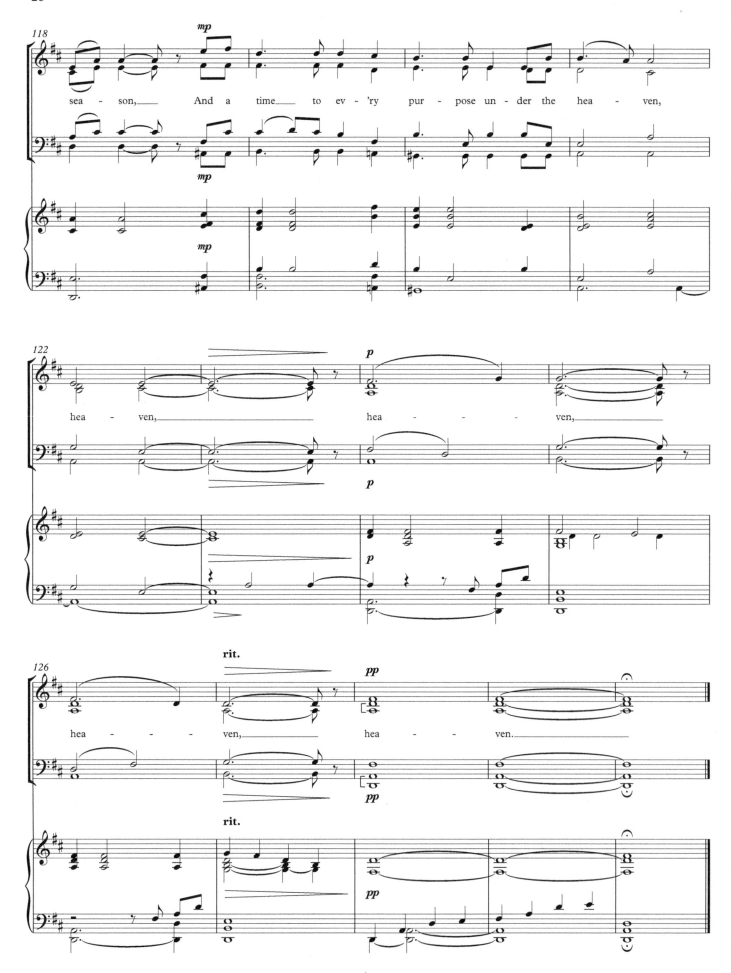

sea - son,_____ And a time____ to ev - 'ry pur - pose un - der the hea - ven,

hea - ven,_____ hea - - - ven,_____

hea - - ven,_____ hea - ven._____

5. Life has loveliness to sell

Sara Teasdale (1884–1933)

Soar - ing fire that sways and sings,_____ And child - ren's fa - ces

look - ing up,_____ Hold - ing won - der in_____ a cup._____

Life has love - li - ness to sell,_____

Mu - sic like a curve of gold, Scent of pine trees

in the rain, Eyes that love you, arms that hold, And

for your spi - rit's still de - light, Ho - ly thoughts that star the

night.

Spend all you have__ for__ love - li - ness,

Buy it and ne - ver count the

cost;_____

For one white sing - ing hour of peace Count

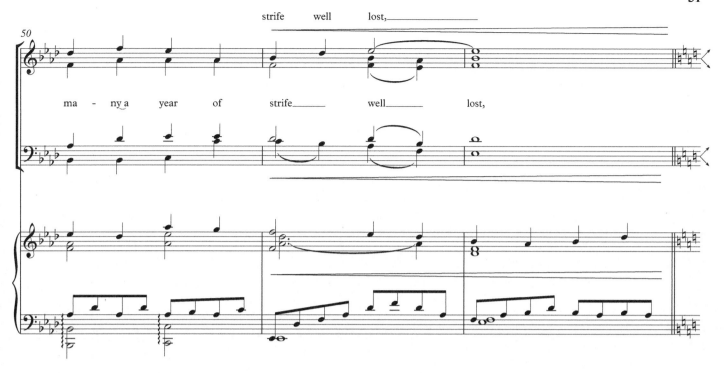

strife well lost,_____

ma - ny a year of strife_____ well_____ lost,

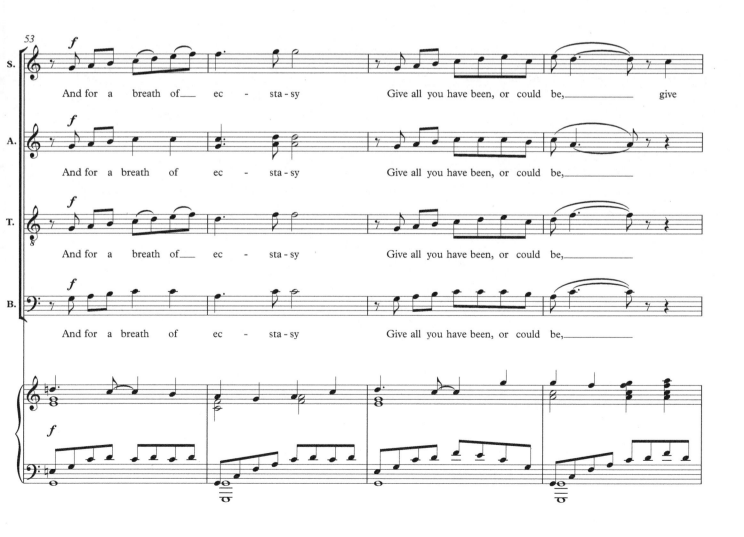

And for a breath of___ ec - sta - sy   Give all you have been, or could be,_____ give

And for a breath of   ec - sta - sy   Give all you have been, or could be,_____

And for a breath of___ ec - sta - sy   Give all you have been, or could be,_____

And for a breath of   ec - sta - sy   Give all you have been, or could be,_____

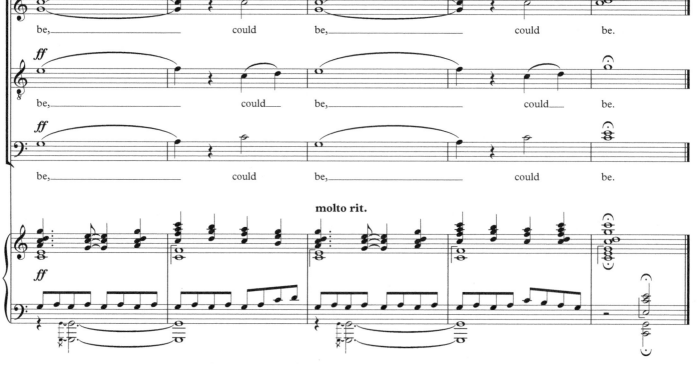